Mindset
Moves
Momentum

Julia A. Royston

BK

ROYSTON
Publishing

BK Royston Publishing
P. O. Box 4321
Jeffersonville, IN 47131
http://www.bkroystonpublishing.com
bkroystonpublishing@gmail.com

Cover Design: Elite Cover Designs
Cover Photo: Jonathan Snorten

ISBN-13: 978-1-959543-85-5

King James Version Scriptural Text – Public Domain

Printed in the United States of America

Dedication

This is dedicated to every one who ever thought about being a business owner. Change your mindset.
Make some moves. Keep going and don't lose your momentum.

Acknowledgements

I thank my Lord and Savior Jesus Christ for giving me another opportunity to introduce more people to you. I thank you that you have for entrusting this gift to me. Lord, let your Spirit move, guide and empower through this book the people who will read it.

To my husband, Brian K. Royston, the love of my life for loving and cheering me on so much that I can be and do all that God has placed in me. I love you.

To my Mom, my greatest supporter and best friend. To my Dad, who is in heaven, whom I know is proud of me and always encouraged me to go for it. Thanks to all the rest of my family for their love and support.

A special thank you to Rev. and Mrs. Claude R. Royston for their love and support.

To the rest of my clients, friends and family, thank you and love you always. Let's go!

Love, Julia

Table of Contents

Introduction

There are so many things that I could write about concerning the last 15 years of being in business. The highs, lows, disappointments, loses and wins but although, that might inspire someone to keep going, know that they are not alone and know that every thing is not perfect in the entrepreneurial world. Secondly, I didn't just want to focus on people writing, publishing or promoting books but that is my first love. As I reflected, I asked myself what are three main things that an entrepreneur should have besides a vision, faith, hard work, favor and God to make it in the marketplace?

Mindset. Moves. Momentum.

Turn the page and let's go to work.

Mindset

For as he thinketh
in his heart, so
is he.

Proverbs 23:7 (KJV)

Mindset

Let this mind be in you, which was also in Christ Jesus.... Philippians 2:5 (KJV)

Where is your mind? What do you think about? What are you focused on? What do you talk about? What do you do? Your mind, your mouth and your movement are all connected. I can't make someone do anything that they really are not ready for. Even if I could talk you into writing a book, guide you through the process and help write it for you, if you are not interested, enjoying it, willing to learn about it and promote it, it won't work, and you won't be successful. Furthermore, you'll always blame me and won't take ownership or responsibility. It's just that simple. I did something at a business conference that I've never done again and that was yell out while someone else was talking or asking a question. The young woman stated that she was having a problem getting her fashion idea/business off the ground. I said that I didn't see any evidence of her having a real interest in fashion, clothing or that industry by her dress, speech or actions online. I said that I eat, drink, sleep and breathe books, writing, publishing and promotion. I had spent thousands of dollars to be a sponsor of the event that I was attending as well as paying for my own travel, etc. I put my money, profits and investment in my dream, goals and business. Where was her investment? If she was interested, show me? The next day at the conference, she had changed her clothing and her speech. I called her on it. As a man thinketh, speaks, walks, invests and performs, so is he and so will he be. To this day and while I am writing this book, that young woman has a very successful fashion coaching and stylist business, connecting with major stores and events for fashion. Her mind, mouth and movement actually connected — along with coaching and accountability — equaled success. Additionally, the thing that you are really mindful of, you will sacrifice for. You will spend money to attend, learn and grow from your interests. You invest in entertainment that you enjoy. You invest in clothing that you like and look good in for events or just every day. You invest in travel, food and other things — why not invest in you?

But first, check your mind. Where is it? What is it focused on that will benefit you in the future? Now I refer to business a lot because that is where my focus is right now in my life, but having the right mindset will help you keep a job, build your family and succeed in life whether you ever start a business, write a book or volunteer at a local charity or non-profit. How you think will affect your whole life. That's important for us all to stop and take a minute to evaluate individually and about ourselves. The old saying, "I can't read your mind," is right but I can tell by what you say and do where your mind is. It is either focused on long-term best practices and goals or only on immediate gratification, right now, go for broke with no thought or nothing left for the future.

I challenge you to search your heart, take note of what's going on in your mind and let your ears be on listening overdrive for what's coming out of your mouth.

Notes

_____

_____

_____

_____

_____

_____

_____

_____

_____

_____

_____

_____

_____

_____

_____

_____

_____

_____

_____

_____

_____

_____

Are you hungry and do you love it?

There are some foods in the world that I love but physically, I can't eat them anymore. On the other hand, there are foods that I will always and thankfully, I will always be able to eat in moderation. Chocolate, steak, lamb chops and pasta. I can't eat these foods every day and must consume some vegetables, etc., to balance it out. These are rich foods and could do damage to my system if I don't enjoy them sparingly. There are some foods that I love but am not hungry for them and won't eat them even if it is on the menu. I don't care how much it costs or if it is a special occasion or if someone else says, "get whatever you want." I still won't order it. I am not hungry for that today or right now or in this season.

Life is not like that. Bills will need to be paid and your family will still need to be supported whether you like it or not. So why not spend your time doing something that drives you and makes you hungry to achieve and do every day? Furthermore, you love it and would do it even if no one paid you. Now that is where I worked to get to in my life. My best life. I still work, hustle, put in the blood, sweat and tears but I love it and am passionate about it. There will be times in life, business, career and ministry where it will be hard, difficult, uncomfortable and you may want to quit but if you love it, you will find a way. If you're hungry enough to stay up late, get up early, work through lunches, sacrifice luxury for practicality, avoid certain situations and people to get it done, you'll succeed. I don't care how much money it made you. The work ethic alone will drive you to the bank. The systematic sacrifice, organization and drive will get you there. Don't worry about where you start and how small the amount of your first invoice was: your path is only up from here. When your mind, mouth and movements all align and you are really hungry for it and love it on top, you'll make it. Let me add this too, that you will have to get some knowledge by reading articles, books and blog posts about your industry. Get a coach, a mentor, go to a class, watch a webinar, get some best practices, put some systems in place, spend some money on graphics, position yourself in places with like-minded people and make presentations or pitch to people who could propel you to the next level, but you'll make it.

What Time Is It?!

And of the children of Issachar, which were men that had understanding of the times, to know what Israel ought to do…. 1 Chronicles 12:32 (KJV)

There will be times when you have to pray, fast and ask God for the time. You can ask Alexa or Siri for the current time, but God knows not of the current time, but the future time and correct time for all things to be done. It may be a good thing and something that you should do in and with your brand. But you need God to tell you the best time to do it. So I ask Him often, what time is it and what should I be doing right now? I have also prayed about doing something that made a lot of sense, and I thought it would be a lot of cents to my budget and bank account, but the time was not right. I even had a client tell me it was not the right time, but I also went to God and prayed about it. He said, "No, not right now." After a few weeks, I realized that God and my client were right. I didn't understand that more clients who needed my regular services would be coming and this new service I couldn't and wouldn't have the time to devote to the work, experimentation or trial and error to it. I didn't have the experience with the new service. I had the knowledge. I had the outsource companies, but it wasn't the right time. I am so glad that I listened. So what time is it? If you don't know, ask the creator of time. Go ask God what time it is.

What should you be focusing your mind on right now and in the season you're in no matter when you're reading this book? There is a time for everything under the heavens.
What time is it?

Mindset to Be an Answer

Bishop Jakes preached a sermon once, "Lord Make Me an Answer." Lord, make me an answer to a question, a solution to a problem or a resource in an information desert. When I travel to different events to present a talk or sell my books or attend a conference to network and learn, I am looking for answers and want to become someone else's answer, solution or resource. I ask people, "what do you need?" I ask people, "what type of book are you looking for and want to read or share with others?" It works for me, and I pray you let it work for you. Why? Because if you find someone who needs what you've got, they'll pay for it if they meet you and trust you. The business motto is that "people do business with those whom they know, like and trust." I know people who don't necessarily like me, but they know me and trust me and are willing to do business with me. I know other people who have known me for years, since I started, but still have never bought anything from me or referred me and never will. If you find people in a room who need what you've got and you deliver in quality and excellence, you've got a client for life. I have a few of these people in my life and I am eternally grateful. Lord, make you and me an answer. Help me to focus my mind to be in the right place, at the right time, saying and doing the right thing to the right person to get them the answer that they need.

Your becoming an answer for the right person is all tied to the connection of your mind, your mouth and your movement. Think about it.

Notes

_____

_____

_____

_____

_____

_____

_____

_____

_____

_____

_____

_____

_____

_____

_____

_____

_____

_____

_____

_____

_____

_____

Notes

_____

_____

_____

_____

_____

_____

_____

_____

_____

_____

_____

_____

_____

_____

_____

_____

_____

_____

_____

_____

_____

Notes

_____

_____

_____

_____

_____

_____

_____

_____

_____

_____

_____

_____

_____

_____

_____

_____

_____

_____

_____

_____

_____

Moves

The steps of a good man are ordered by the Lord.

Psalm 37:23 (KJV)

Moves

Divine Moves

Acknowledge the Lord in all your ways. Now I don't know if you are a person of faith or not, but I can't live without *God in My Business*. Yes, that is one of my book titles but also something that I live by. I have made mistakes, and He allowed me to make them, but there are some moves I can truthfully say are "Divine Moves" or moves that God, Himself, told me to make. These are normally moves that don't make sense to anyone but Him. These are moves that happen at times when the greatest, best and happiest times are happening in my life, but He said, "Go now or shut that down now or resign for that position now or quit that job now." When I did it when He said, it looked crazy, and I was thought of as crazy. Later on, people have asked me, "how did you know to do that right then?" I told them that God said do it and I did it. I wish I had a magic formula to give to you about these moves, but I don't. I can tell you that I didn't earn or deserve God's move or favor, but He allowed it to happen to me and I'm thankful. For those of you reading this, seek God in faith and sincerity, and He will answer you. The seeking has to be on purpose and for His purpose. For your own personal gain only, and not to move the

Kingdom, benefit anyone else, help someone else, lead someone out of a horrible situation or that God will get the glory, won't work. Now, it may work for a short time, but long term, it will fail every time. What you reap, you will sow.

Your Moves

What are your moves? Where should you be? What should you be doing? What is your real business? Sorry, but I'm going to say, are you minding your business or basing your business on what others are doing? The moves a person makes with four children under the age of 10 and the moves someone makes as a retiree, with grown children with successful, sustainable careers are totally different. The Bible tells us, "comparing yourself to others is NOT wise." Don't do it. Determine what you should be doing, love to do, have a gifting to do, talent to do, and people are asking you to help them do the same thing. Those are the moves that you should be making. I've said it over and over again — business owner, entrepreneur, being on your hustle and grind is NOT for everyone. Do you have the heart for it? Do you have the desire to keep going when things aren't going well? Do you even enjoy it and want to spend time learning, growing and doing it better even when people aren't paying you? Those should be your moves. Not mine but your moves. I have someone right now whom I am mentoring and coaching to publish books for herself and others. Over time, I realize that the way that she will approach her business will be totally different from how I run my business. Why? First of all, it will be her business and not mine no matter how much I advise her. Her name and reputation will be associated with the business, not mine. Second, her experience is different from mine. I've been doing this for 15+ years and still don't know all I need to know. She will be starting from scratch and will make many mistakes and misjudgments along the way. I did and I'll try to help her avoid some but there are some things that you can't avoid but can only learn through doing, good or bad.

My challenge to you is to sit down and determine what you really should be doing right now in your life, career and/or business? Do that thing that keeps you up late at night, wakes you up early and you literally jump out of the bed to get to in the morning.

Social Media Moves

This statement is not to criticize anyone on social media because I, myself, post every single day and pay someone to post and/or share my advertisements each month. So I am not criticizing anyone for social media. Social media is a resource, a tool, a platform that is not mine, but I utilize it for the growth, development and reach of my business. Social media is NOT my BOSS. I am still a business woman, so I do know how many friends I have. I know how many likes my live streams get. I know about graphics that have gotten a lot of views, hits or shares. I know when there is crickets or silence when I post. More importantly, I keep "the main thing" the main thing. For me it is about literacy, writing, publishing and promotion of my books, author client books and people whom I didn't publish but represent their books at events or online. I also travel extensively and meet people who have watched me, follow me and can tell me what I'm doing, and I've seen them on a live stream, like or share any posts of mine; they're still watching me move. So business wise, I give them something to see, learn, grow and know. I congratulate others on their wins and share books on my social media platform by authors whom I publish and some I don't publish. If the Lord be my helper and keeper, I don't want to sell out, embarrass myself for a like or a share on social media. I have too many people whom I meet who follow me, buy books from and eventually recommend me as a publisher to others without it. I don't talk about every place I go, every person I meet, every meal I eat or everything I buy or how I live. Unless it will be helpful and beneficial to my business, it doesn't need to be said. Do I have pictures? Of course. I am a librarian by training, so I keep a journal, portfolio of every city, state, event or vacation that I've been on, but you won't see many of the events online. It's not necessary or beneficial to my brand or business or life. There are some things I am going to look back, remember, look at the picture or view the video when I don't want to work this hard anymore. It is personal. It is private. It was not for public consumption or criticism. Decide today how you want to live your life and make social media moves online. It can be helpful or harmful. There are people who screenshot all types of images that you post online and even if you delete them from your social media page, they can pull them up from their cloud storage, phone or backup drives. Don't play out in the Internet streets. It can be dangerous.

I have been teased often and I've written about it before, that my social media posts are filled with encouragement, enrichment and empowerment. I plan to keep it that way.

My challenge to you is to go back through your social media posts and take a quick look. What do you see? Are they something that you would share with your great- grandmother? Would your children and future generations be proud of what you posted? Then reconsider your next social media post before you hit post, send or share.

Loud Moves

I am the Queen of "Happy Birthday" or "Congratulations" or "Awesome" or "Happy Anniversary" or "Come through, Gorgeous" or just a "Yes!" I genuinely love to see people win, look nice or achieve the smallest thing in their life. They are trying, progressing, accomplishing or achieving things in their life and I am happy about it. Major milestones in my life, business and career, I do make loud moves on social media, my email list or a live stream. I am proud of myself and want others to celebrate with me. Others will not be happy for me but that's okay because you will still see and know it. More importantly than people, I want the devil to see me celebrate because he didn't want me to win, tried to stop me with attacks in the spirit, illness, through people or doubt within myself, but I still made it. Loud moves such as attending events, speaking engagements and/or live streams or interviews, give people more opportunity to meet you, hear your perspective, ask you questions online and feel your spirit out or personality to see if they want to support you in any way. These days because there are so many books and authors out there, for every $10 spent toward any book I write, I am greatly appreciative. People don't have to support you at all. These loud moves are also milestones for people watching who may want to connect, partner or work with me. It shows a sign of credibility, accountability and sustainability. Now, let me caution us all and say that there are liars, deceivers and scammers out there but vet everyone, ask for references, ask plenty of questions, keep watching, go slow or small before you spend a great deal of your budget and possibly lose time or money.

My challenge to you is make loud moves. Be ready for those that don't agree, approve or acknowledge the move. Be ready for some people not to speak, congratulate you or be in your circle again. That's okay because they weren't meant for your next move; this is their stop and they get off here.

Move in Silence

There are some moves that you don't need to announce on social media, your email list, on a call, live stream, notecard, just nothing at all. Just move. Because I was raised in a house where my parents were entrepreneurs in the evening but my dad was a teacher in the daytime, I knew about what to tell people and what not to tell people about my life, business, money and career. My dad just made moves with my mom's help and support. They both worked in key positions in ministry at our church, but we didn't discuss what we did at home with most people at church. No announcement. No loud move, just moving. Some moves that can have an effect on multiple people should receive a notification in some way, shape or form. I recently had another company contacting my clients about doing business with them. There were so many questions, I needed to notify my clients that I didn't send them, endorse them or approve of them. If they work with them, be sure and vet them, ask questions and move at your own risk not holding me or any of my businesses liable. No contract or agreement we had would prevent them from doing business with this other company, but I don't know them. That's a situation where you can't move in silence. I didn't announce it on social media: my clients got an email from me. Several thanked me and were appreciative that I warned them.

My moves in silence are different from others because my business is different from other businesses. If I had a brick and mortar store where I kept specific business hours, I would need to announce everywhere that we would be closed on these days, times and locations. But I am mobile, virtual and can do business literally anywhere in the world with a good battery and Internet access. If you want to have a conversation, you get on my calendar. If my calendar is blocked off for a few days or weeks, I don't need to announce it on social media or go live about it, I just block off the days. It's just that simple. When my father passed away in 2010, people were understanding and respectful of a specific grieving time to pass before I would be working again. Adults understand. Adults with immature behavior or needs, wouldn't understand. Did I go off the grid for 6 months or not respond to an email, text or DM for weeks or months? No — because I still had a business to run. Did I need a couple of weeks? Of course — and those who understood were fine with it. When I had COVID and was in the hospital, I struggled, but a young lady had paid me in full for a book and I was still working on it while in the hospital. When I notified her that I might be a little late and here is why, she said to stop working and get better, that she was fine and when I was ready she would have her book released. On oxygen and in a hospital bed, I finished the book, and she got her book on time. Why? My name and business reputation were on the line. My health was a priority, too, but I willed my way to the finish line. That move didn't need to be broadcast to anyone but her, my client. A move in silence that was a powerful move for her life, my business and brand.

Network/Industry Moves

I'm different in that I will interview, go live and be on platforms with people who are in the same business that I am in. These are network/industry moves for me. Why? Because there are very few black faces that are major players in the literary, publishing and writing world. I want that to be seen and heard. I want our experiences, expertise and businesses spotlighted and highlighted. I have had so many people ask me why I do that or how that works for me in the end. First, I don't worry about how that will benefit me. My objective is to be a facilitator to introduce people to the market, industry, structure, ideas, processes and systems of the literary industry. There are more than nine billion people on the planet. As much as people admire how many books I've written and published, I will not be publishing nine billion books. I am getting tired just thinking about it. But do I need to encourage, inspire and warn people about what to do and what NOT to do when publishing their books. Absolutely. Should I be a proponent of telling future and potential authors what the hottest trends, changing in the major publishing outlet and how they can generate or retain more sales and profits with their books? Absolutely.

Secondly, I believe that there are enough clients, books, opportunities and money for all of us to eat, thrive and win. Finally, I have never spotlighted, been on anyone else's platform, promoted someone else's book, publishing company, literary agency or event and not been blessed to have a new client, event or opportunity come my way. It's a law. You reap what you sow.

Move Differently

So he went another way, and returned not by the way that he came to Bethel.
1 Kings 13:10 (KJV)

Sometimes God will tell you specifically what to do and how to move. At times, He will tell you to move, stop, go in another direction, do something new or pause and rest. He has the master plan. I Kings 13 is the story of a prophet carrying out orders from God. (Read the entire chapter.) He was told specifically that when he returned from the place that God told him to go, he was instructed to NOT go in the same direction back but to go another way home. Do not take the same path, same direction, same streets or same highway home as you came. Most of the time we want to take the easiest way, shortest distance and least complicated way to get home. If you're like me, the streets are crazy, so I want to get home as fast and an easy as possible. BUT there could be a reason — and only God sees that reason — that you need to go in a different direction: a drunk driver, a distracted driver, a detour, a traffic jam or other construction that could stop you from getting home safety.

In your business, there may be times that it will look as if you should be going in a specific direction, doing a specific thing like everyone else especially those in your industry but make sure that you listen to God and be willing to move differently. Move the way He wants you to move. Do what He tells you to do as He tells you to do it, and you will reap the benefit. Sometimes it's not always money.

Sometimes it's the act of obedience. Sometimes it will be access to something or someone that you are divinely directed to so that your business, career, life and purpose are benefited. We need money. We like money and we love what money can do, but sometimes we need information, access and people to get to the next level and NOT just money.

Before Your Next Move

Recently, I heard the Lord say, before you make a move in this next season, determine whether it will be an introduction, information or income. Some events and moves have been all three. But others have been an introduction: I gathered much information — which at times can be priceless — but the income was very minimal. My husband is great with money and always wants me to be as profitable as possible. Over time, he has learned that some things are for the long-term game; other events are introductory, and I am putting the brand in front of people who are just meeting me and may not be ready to make an investment of any kind right away but over time, they will see my investment and spend with me over and over again. I always have to warn him before I go to new places because he used to see people doing business with us as buying a book or being interested in publishing. I am thankful and grateful, but on the other hand, there are other events where I am there to learn. It cost me to get in the room, but the education will inspire me to go home, regroup, plot out my next move, strategize, get advice from others, have ZOOM calls and send some thank you gift cards. It works. I am thankful and don't mind showing it for the lessons I've learned and people who have helped me along the way. So before you read on and accept my next two challenges, decide whether the job, career move, business opportunity, grant application, the new product you're creating or the potential client you'll be working with or the next collaboration event that you will participate in is for introduction, information or income. Let's go!

My challenge to you is whom can you partner, collaborate or help sponsor an event with? Make sure that it is a win/win situation but if two or three will touch and agree…. I'll let you finish that statement and biblical principle.

My final challenge in this chapter is this: what are your next moves? Whom do you need to connect with? What's the purpose, goal, people, and what will be the result? Is this move for money or for legacy? Is this move for business placement, positioning and platform or just a time to show off to your friends and family? Think about the investment of time, energy, money and effort, is it worth it or what will be the return on that investment? I have invested much in projects or events and got a huge educational, learning and lesson return and not money. Think about it before you launch that next thing, project, idea or product.

*Month*_____

Goals_____

_____

_____

_____

_____

_____

Due Date(s)_____

_____

_____

Resources Needed

_____

_____

_____

_____

_____

Resources in House

_____

_____

_____

_____

_____

*Month*_____

Goals_____

_____

_____

_____

_____

_____

Due Date(s)_____

_____

_____

Resources Needed

_____

_____

_____

_____

_____

Resources in House

_____

_____

_____

_____

*Month*_____

Goals_____

_____

_____

_____

_____

_____

Due Date(s)_____

_____

_____

Resources Needed

_____

_____

_____

_____

_____

Resources in House

_____

_____

_____

_____

_____

*Month*_____

Goals_____

_____

_____

_____

_____

_____

Due Date(s)_____

_____

_____

Resources Needed

_____

_____

_____

_____

_____

Resources in House

_____

_____

_____

_____

_____

*Month*_____

Goals_____

_____

_____

_____

_____

Due Date(s)_____

_____

_____

Resources Needed

_____

_____

_____

_____

_____

Resources in House

_____

_____

_____

_____

_____

*Month*_____

Goals_____

_____

_____

_____

_____

_____

Due Date(s)_____

_____

_____

Resources Needed

_____

_____

_____

_____

_____

Resources in House

_____

_____

_____

_____

_____

Month_____

Goals_____

_____

_____

_____

_____

Due Date(s)_____

_____

_____

Resources Needed

_____

_____

_____

_____

Resources in House

_____

_____

_____

_____

_____

*Month*_____

Goals_____

_____

_____

_____

_____

_____

Due Date(s)_____

_____

_____

Resources Needed

_____

_____

_____

_____

_____

Resources in House

_____

_____

_____

_____

_____

*Month*_____

Goals_____

_____

_____

_____

_____

Due Date(s)_____

_____

_____

Resources Needed

_____

_____

_____

_____

_____

Resources in House

_____

_____

_____

_____

_____

*Month*_____

Goals_____
_____
_____
_____
_____
_____

Due Date(s)_____
_____
_____

Resources Needed

_____
_____
_____
_____
_____

Resources in House

_____
_____
_____
_____
_____

*Month*_____

Goals_____

_____

_____

_____

_____

_____

Due Date(s)_____

_____

_____

Resources Needed

_____

_____

_____

_____

_____

Resources in House

_____

_____

_____

_____

_____

*Month*_____

Goals_____

_____

_____

_____

_____

_____

Due Date(s)_____

_____

_____

Resources Needed

_____

_____

_____

_____

_____

Resources in House

_____

_____

_____

_____

_____

Notes

_____

_____

_____

_____

_____

_____

_____

_____

_____

_____

_____

_____

_____

_____

_____

_____

_____

_____

_____

_____

_____

Momentum

**And David
enquired at the
LORD, saying,
Shall I pursue
after this troop?
shall I overtake
them? And he
answered him,
Pursue**

1 Samuel 30:8 (KJV)

Momentum

Momentum is defined as force or speed of movement; impetus, as of a physical object or course of events, www.dictionary.com.

When I worked a full-time job during the day, worked a part-time job in the evenings, cleaned two buildings for my dad's cleaning service and led worship at a church on Sunday, my business didn't get enough attention and the movement in my business was slow. At this time, I sang more than anything. I hadn't written my first book or married Brian Royston. It was prophesied to me that my ministry and business would take off once I was married. I was tired but liked the idea of next level, a husband to help and God's favor on my life. Now, I realize that I couldn't gain momentum in what God called me to do because I was helping build, drive or support other people's businesses, ministries and careers. These endeavors gave me money to pay bills, thank the Lord, but this was my real purpose, passion and position. These were resources to get me to a place and in position for what God really called me to do. But I couldn't stop; I had to keep going even though I really didn't know where I was going or who my husband was or what the end goal really was going to look like. I had to keep going. In the new place where I was, like Ruth, I was being seen, utilized and opportunities were presenting themselves for me to be in position and on larger platforms. My gift was truly making room for me, but it still didn't feel like this was mine. I was still helping others. Back then, it didn't really matter to me. I was good with helping others. But God was really moving me toward what He wanted me to do, be, grow and along with my husband, lead. When I look back now, it makes sense. These were the training, educating and expansion years. But these times were hard because I was walking away from what was familiar into a true faith walk of the unfamiliar. If I am honest, most of my life, I was taught again being in the company of the people whom God was leading me directly to. These were the hardest years of my life. More than college, more than a divorce, more than no friends and a low-paying job, leaving the familiar was the hardest. My core, immediate family had my back no matter what, but they didn't understand. My extended family loved me but were totally confused as well. My friends and associates just forsook me. What do you do? You cry, pray, work and keep moving. You hear God's voice, know that He is with you and keep moving. You get prophesies, receive strength, meet new people who speak life into you and keep moving. The pace was slow. The road was dark. The victories were many but not as joyous because I felt like I was with strangers and not the familiar. Over time, with God's help, the strangers became family, friends and the support I needed in what seemed like a new world. I kept moving. Others forgot me and no longer called, but others met me for the first time and moved me to the front of the line, sat me on the front row, introduced me, preferred me, and God favored and blessed me. It was the best and worst time of my life all at the same time. It was scary, but God made it a time where I needed Him more than ever. I had never been this way before. I didn't know the way. Nothing was familiar. Each step I needed assurance and reassurance that I was going the right way, with the right people and doing the right thing. It was an incredible experience. I don't consider myself a natural risk taker, maverick or trailblazer. I am a great follower but this time, I had to be trained to be the leader. With tears, setbacks, disappointments, rejection and fear, I never lost my momentum. I had to keep going. I didn't have a go back to go back to. There was no way to go but forward. There was no time but now, and I didn't have a map but had to wait on God's voice to start, stop, turn right or go left. I still live like this to this day. Through sickness, my father's death, my husband's sickness, my doubts and fears, no support, great support, I didn't lose my momentum. It is keeping me alive. Some days are slow. Some days are fast. Some days are filled with wins and some days I see so many losses I want to stop but I keep going. I don't want to lose my momentum. The goal may or may not be reached today but you don't want to be caught doing nothing to even keep going or obtain that goal or finish that project with greater intensity or achievement if you do nothing. Never. Keep going. Keep moving.

Life Will Keep on "Lifeing"

I see people online or in person that literally stop because life has been doing so much lifeing. Is "lifeing" a word? Oh well, that's the best way I can describe it. Death, sickness, betrayal, abandonment, disappointment, little help, liars, cheaters and haters but that's life. What are you going to do about it? You can't stop certain things from happening. You can't control it. You can only control you. You can only determine how you think, feel and move. Keep moving. Make adjustments to the goal. Don't announce it but you may have to cut back on some expenses, stop offering some services, downsize, do a virtual rather than an in-person event, get up earlier, stay up a little later but don't lose your momentum. Keep going. Why? Because it is so much harder to build momentum back up once you've started going. My parents' house is on the top of a hill. When we first moved into the house, there was little traffic on our street, and my sisters and I could ride our bikes down the hill with great speed. But coming back up the hill, we would have to gain a lot of speed at the bottom of the hill to propel us back to the top of the hill where our house was. If you didn't pump fast enough to have enough momentum to get up the hill, it would be too hard to pedal, and sometimes I would have to just get off the bike and push it up the hill and start over. That's what I'm warning you about, the start-over part. It's so much harder when you have to completely start over.

Keep your email list. Keep your online store and keep sending out emails to people who have supported you in the past. If you are taking care of an elderly parent and can't travel, go online, promote it online, ship the product out from your house. Arrange postal pick-ups, coordinate runs with a temporary service. Do drop shipping through Amazon or another online service but don't lose all of your momentum and have to start all over because starting again from the bottom is hard. Now if you can't help it and you do have to start all over, I get it and totally understand but at least, work smarter the next time. Don't burn bridges. Notify whoever you need to notify and keep up relationships. Explain to your manufacturers and suppliers what's going on and make arrangements. Tell your real clients what your new services are now and how you can be reached. Offer a discount when you do come back for those who were loyal while you get your true momentum back. I don't want to see you like me, running alongside of a bike, business or career that you should be riding on and now you're pushing with all of your might to get up a hill that a few months ago you were laughing, happy with a smile on your face and a pep in your step all of the way to the bank.

You may have to decrease your business model and services, but don't decrease your business intensity or quality. I see businesses do it all of the time, they change their times of operation by having later hours in the summer and shorter hours in the winter, but don't decrease your quality of customer service, product presentation or delivery. During

COVID, there were some restaurants that you could only order at the window and couldn't come in. Their procedures changed but they still were able to operate. The menu items or services that some businesses offer may not be available and just seasonal. One of my favorite ice cream shops closes in October and reopens in February. They are not opened in November, December and January. Can you only operate three days a week or after 4 p.m. every day or four days a week or only take private clients or only do group coaching? What does that look like for you? I've seen businesses start out as a food truck and then open a restaurant. Some people with restaurants have food trucks temporarily or for special events. For me, I am the queen of vending events. I travel all of the time, but can I do that year round? Sometimes I can, but if it snows or there is an ice storm, I'm in the house, online, live streaming and promoting my products and services. I don't want to lose my momentum. I don't want to go off of the scene for months at a time and then try to get that bike back up the hill.

Momentum also propels you to the next opportunity or position. As I said my parents' house was on a hill, but when we got down our hill, there was another hill that would take us down or up another hill. It was a constant fun time on a bike. Just like life, there are hills, valleys, low times and fun times at different times. But you need the high times to get you through the low times. You need the laughter to help you get through the tears. You need to save some money so when you're short, you have the extra to carry you through.

You may have to pause, reset, regroup, take a breather but get back on that bike, horse, computer, laptop, platform and keep going. Don't lose your momentum.

Notes

_____

_____

_____

_____

_____

_____

_____

_____

_____

_____

_____

_____

_____

_____

_____

_____

_____

_____

_____

_____

_____

Conclusion

You have to be mature, ask questions, seek helpful advice, pray, fast, meditate, read and decide how you want to live your life. It's your decision.

When I first wanted to write this book, I wanted to focus on the term and service "Book Business Boss ^{tm}." I am still after two years striving to get the trademark for Book Business Boss, but it remains in application phase. Only God knows why. I digress, but I realize that I didn't want to focus the book for just authors or people interested in writing a book and being a boss at the literacy game but being a boss at life. The boss of your life and who God created you to be and what He has gifted you to do in the earth and for the world!

So I have three statements and then an acronym to help you on your journey.

1. You either have something to say or not. It is your decision.
2. Don't stop striving until you're living the life that God intended for you to live. This should not be based on anyone else's definition of success or achievement but your own.
3. Make sure that you have life, business and family systems in

place to support, anchor, grow and sustain the life that you've built.

What is a boss in my estimation?

The **B** stands for a Belief System. What do you believe in about yourself and your life?

The **O** stands for Outstanding Character for Big Dreams

The **S** stands for Servant Worth Ethic

The other **S** stands for Student for Life

That's a real **BOSS** in my opinion. If you need help, let's have a conversation at

www.talkwithroyston.com. Let's go!

Notes

_____

_____

_____

_____

_____

_____

_____

_____

_____

_____

_____

_____

_____

_____

_____

_____

_____

_____

_____

_____

_____

_____

Notes

_____

_____

_____

_____

_____

_____

_____

_____

_____

_____

_____

_____

_____

_____

_____

_____

_____

_____

_____

_____

Notes

_____

_____

_____

_____

_____

_____

_____

_____

_____

_____

_____

_____

_____

_____

_____

_____

_____

_____

_____

_____

_____

_____

_____

Notes

Notes

_____

_____

_____

_____

_____

_____

_____

_____

_____

_____

_____

_____

_____

_____

_____

_____

_____

_____

_____

_____

_____

_____

Notes

_____

_____

_____

_____

_____

_____

_____

_____

_____

_____

_____

_____

_____

_____

_____

_____

_____

_____

_____

_____

Notes

_____

_____

_____

_____

_____

_____

_____

_____

_____

_____

_____

_____

_____

_____

_____

_____

_____

_____

_____

_____

Notes

_____

_____

_____

_____

_____

_____

_____

_____

_____

_____

_____

_____

_____

_____

_____

_____

_____

_____

_____

_____

_____

_____

About the Author

Julia Royston spends her days doing what she loves: writing, publishing, speaking and coaching others to write and monetize their messages to the world.

"Helping You Get Your Message to the Masses and Turn Your Words into Wealth," that is her why and motto. To date, Julia has written 88+ books, published 400+, recorded 3 music CDs and coached more than 250 "to be" published authors in the book business. She is the owner of five companies, a non-profit organization, editor of the Book Business Boss Magazine as well as the host of "Live Your Best Life" heard each Sunday morning at 10:00 a.m. EST and "The Book Business Boss Show" on Tuesdays 10:30 a.m. EST on www.envision-radio.com and a contributing author to Envision Radio Magazine.

To stay connected with Julia, visit www.juliaakroyston.com.

Social Media

Facebook — @juliaaroyston

IG — @juliaaroyston

LinkedIn — @juliaaroyston

TikTok — @juliaaroyston

Other Books by This Author

Julia Royston Books
www.juliaroystonstore.com

Julia Royston Books
www.juliaroystonstore.com

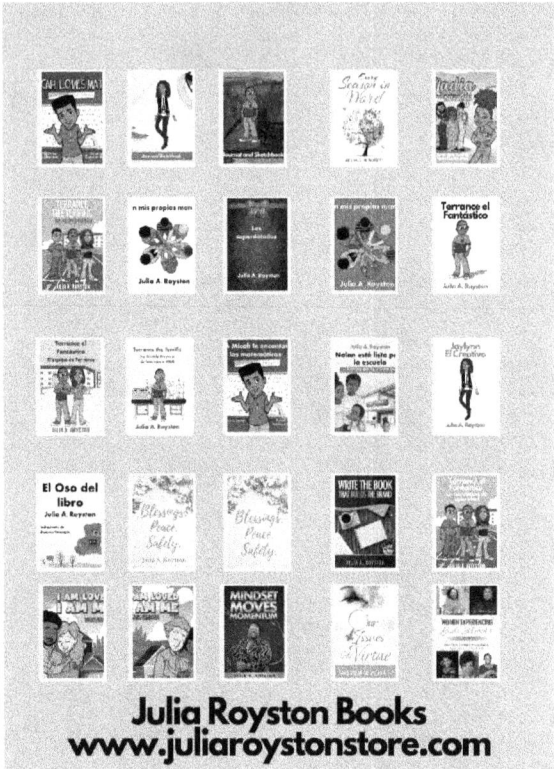

Julia Royston Books
www.juliaroystonstore.com

www.ingramcontent.com/pod-product-compliance
Lightning Source LLC
Chambersburg PA
CBHW071459200326
41519CB00019B/5802